30 Minutes ... To Succeed in Business Writing

Graham Hart

KOGAN PAGE

First Indian Edition 1997
Reprinted 2003, 2008

Kogan Page India Private Limited
4737/23 Ansari Road,
Daryaganj
New Delhi 110 002

ISBN-10: 81-7554-071-0
ISBN-13: 978-81-7554-071-2

Published by Vinod Vasishtha for Kogan Page India Private Limited, 4737/23 Ansari Road, Daryaganj, New Delhi - 110 002.

Printed and bound at Print Perfect, New Delhi - 110 064.

CONTENTS

The 30 Minutes Series

The Kogan Page 30 Minutes Series has been devised to give your confidence a boost when faced with tackling a new skill or challenge for the first time.

So the next time you're thrown in at the deep end and want to bring your skills up to scratch or pep up your career prospects, turn to the *30 Minutes Series* for help!

Titles available are:
30 Minutes Before A Meeting
30 Minutes Before A Presentation
30 Minutes to Boost Your Communication Skills
30 Minutes to Boost Your Self Esteem
30 Minutes to Brainstorm Great Ideas
30 Minutes to Deal With Difficult People
30 Minutes to Get Your Own Way
30 Minutes to Get Promoted
30 Minutes to Improve Your Networking Skills
30 Minutes to Make the Right Decision
30 Minutes to Manage Your Time Better
30 Minutes to Market Yourself
30 Minutes to Master the Internet
30 Minutes to Motivate Your Staff
30 Minutes to Negotiate a Better Deal
30 Minutes to Plan a Project
30 Minutes to Solve that Problem
30 Minutes to Succeed in Business Writing
30 Minutes to Write a Business Plan
30 Minutes to Write a Marketing Plan
30 Minutes to Write a Report
30 Minutes to Write Sales Letters

Available from all good bookseller.
For further information on the series, please contact:

Kogan Page India Private Limited
2/13, Ansari Road, Daryaganj, New Delhi-110 002
Tel. 23258325, 23279280, 23283121, 23285874, Fax 0091 11 23267224

1. How to get the best from this book

This book provides a guide to the basic skills required for successful business writing. It is probably best to begin at the beginning and work your way through.

Remember that you and I are involved in the process of communication. In your work you will be trying to communicate with your customers and colleagues. This book will provide you with an introduction to all the skills you require. It is up to you, however, how you use them. You will constantly have to ask yourself questions. Is this the tone I wish to use? Is this point explained clearly? Is there a rule I should be following here?

You may even end up asking yourself whether a written communication is best. Should you telephone instead? Should you draw a diagram? This book will provide you with the set of skills you need to be able to make those decisions.

If you do not have a house style document to work to you should use a standard dictionary. Not only will this help you with spellings and meaning but it will also ensure consistency in areas such as hyphenation and capitalisation.

2. Think before you begin

You should always think about the purpose of any type of writing – but especially business writing. Ask yourself the following questions:

What are you writing about?
It is very easy to begin a writing task without considering exactly what you need to include. You may waste your time by having to edit later, or send your client or colleague information they do not need.

Who is the recipient?
Exactly who is going to read your communication? Is it an internal or external client? Will the person who receives it show it to others? Will the recipient understand technical terms? Can the tone be informal?

Why are you undertaking the task?
Do you wish to provide information? Do you wish to persuade or influence the recipient? What type of response are you anticipating? Answers to these questions help you select the style and form of your communication.

How are you going to communicate?

> Put yourself in the place of the recipient. How would you feel if you received a letter? A fax? Or an e-mail? Would you have preferred a phone call?

3. What type of writing?

You have decided, broadly, the answers to the questions 'What', 'Who' and 'Why'. Because all business communications have a specific purpose, it is worth spending a moment or two more considering the question 'Why'.

Why are you spending your valuable time writing to this person or company? What is the intended purpose of your communication? Perhaps you wish to inform somebody, or to influence somebody.

- Writing that is intended purely to inform can be called **Effective Writing**.
- Writing that is intended to influence readers can be called **Writing for Effect**.

Effective Writing means using the simplest possible constructions and styles to convey basic facts. The sole intention of Effective Writing is to send information. Writing for Effect means trying to bring somebody around to your way of thinking. This type of writing may be a letter or report, or might comprise advertisements or slogans.

Most writing tasks will fall somewhere between the two. If you understand, approximately, where you stand between the two extremes you will know immediately what skills to employ, what tone to use and what vocabulary to use.

> The whole process of thinking need only take a few moments. These are important questions, but it is not intended that you spend a lot of time on them.

4. The basic rules

The stadium planning meeting will be held at 2.00 pm on 4 November 1997. The venue is the client's conference suite, where coffee will be served from 1.30 pm. I suggest we meet there at 1.45 pm. This will give us a few minutes to discuss crucial points. Please call to confirm this arrangement.

This is simple, effective writing. The meaning is absolutely clear. The writer has successfully communicated a few simple facts and requested one action from the recipient. The tone is businesslike. The communication took very little time to write and even less time to read. Writing like this is extremely cost-effective.

You need to produce effective writing, as above, for two reasons:

- to communicate simply and quickly

- to establish a good base for developing more advanced writing styles.

It is important to follow the five key rules which produce good, effective business communications:

✔ use simple words when simple words will do

✔ use simple constructions, with the key point first

✔ make each sentence self-contained – as far as possible

✔ use a sentence for one main concept only

✔ write in the active voice.

These rules are explained in more detail on the following pages.

5. Simple words when simple words will do

Short, common words which are easy to read and understand should form the basis of effective business writing. Never use complex words unless you have to. Your writing will be more difficult to understand and may also sound pompous and old-fashioned.

Sometimes longer words are unavoidable – technical terms, product or place names and complex words specifically related to your business activities. The key part of the rule, therefore, is to use simple words *when simple words will do*.

Consider the following list:

What it says …	*What it means …*
ascertain	find out
commencement	start

concerning	about
endeavour	try
foremost	first
initiate	begin
notwithstanding	despite
particulars	facts
pertaining to	about
remuneration	pay
sufficient	enough
supplementary	extra

Beware, also, of 'extending' words. These longer forms may cause confusion as they often have a slightly different meaning. Examples include:

event	⇨	eventuality
documents	⇨	documentation
use	⇨	usage
method	⇨	methodology
expenses	⇨	expenditure

The advice on this page does not mean that longer words should *never* be used – but think carefully about them. If in doubt, always choose the simple option.

6. Simple constructions, with the key point first

You should aim to get to the point quickly in a sentence, making the meaning clear as soon as possible. Achieve this using simple sentence constructions, starting, wherever possible, with the key element.

These examples show good and bad practice.

The meeting will be held in the client's conference suite. ✔

The reader will read the word 'meeting' first. This introduces the topic, so that the reader is ready for information related to this topic.

The client's conference suite is the venue for the meeting. ✘

This sentence is not incorrect, but it is not as effective as the earlier version. The reader will note that something is taking place; what it is will not immediately be clear. The key point is the meeting, not the conference suite. Here are two more examples to consider:

Company policy is to ensure the highest quality, at the lowest possible cost, in every area of our services. ✔
Ensuring the highest quality, at the lowest possible cost, in every area of our services, is the company policy. ✘

Juliette Smith has rejoined Plenith UK as marketing director; she was previously sales manager, before spending the last two years working in the USA. ✔
Now back from the USA where she has been working for the past two years, Juliette Smith has rejoined Plenith UK as marketing director; she was previously sales manager. ✘

This last example could be used in a situation where you were making a point about the USA, but in most situations Juliette Smith should be the key starting point.

7. Self-contained sentences – as far as possible

Try to recall how you read business communications. Do you begin at the beginning and work methodically through to the end? Probably not. Most of us 'skim read' documents looking for key points. Sometimes we return to a letter or document, re-reading certain sections.

For this reason (and others) it is important to make sure as many of your sentences as possible are self-contained. This means that each sentence should work alone, without needing the preceding or following sentence to set it in context. Here are some examples:

The absence of a delivery note (or a copy of one) suggests that we did not receive the photographs. ✔

The absence of a delivery note (or a copy of one) suggests that we did not receive them. ✘

This is much later than we would have wished. ✘

In both the second and third examples the problem occurs with the 'pronoun'. The pronouns 'them' and 'This' stand in the place of other words (nouns) and it is not clear to what they refer.

> Remember that this rule includes the proviso 'as far as possible'. This is not an easy rule to follow all the time.

8. A sentence for one main concept only

Sentences containing one main concept or theme are easy to read. The main point is clear and easy to remember. Remember, however, that this rule applies to concepts, not facts. Even very simple sentences can contain more than one fact. These examples demonstrate the difference:

The purchase price is reasonable and affordable. ✔

This sentence tells us that the purchase price is reasonable. It also tells us that the purchase price is affordable. We now know two facts (or possibly opinions) about the purchase price. There is only one main concept.

The purchase price is reasonable and affordable and the building is situated alongside the main railway station. ✘

The writer in this sentence wants to provide information about both the price and the location – two concepts. One piece of information may obscure the other. Two separate sentences would be better.

Sometimes, of course, you will have closely linked concepts. Consider this example:

The purchase price is reasonable and the company should make an immediate bid. ✔

> If you have to deal with closely linked concepts, you must decide how much emphasis you want to give each of them. See how the sentences fit with the rest of the communication. You can use one or two sentences. The golden rule, if in doubt, again is to keep it simple.

9. Write in the active voice

The best way to illustrate the difference between the active and passive voice is with two simple examples:

The company won the contract. (ACTIVE)

The contract was won by the company. (PASSIVE)

You should always be looking for the most direct, or active, form of the verb – the word that is 'doing' the action. Active verbs inevitably make the writing more dynamic and easier to understand. Sometimes you will convert a passive into an active, and discover an even simpler way of expressing yourself:

A payment was made by the company last Wednesday. ✗
The company made a payment last Wednesday. ✓
The company paid last Wednesday. ✓✓

> Except in special circumstances, always aim to use proper sentences containing a verb. Readers are used to this and will find the style easy to understand.

10. Using punctuation

Try not to think of punctuation as a necessary evil. Think of its:

- *practical use* – as a series of signposts to readers, indicating where ideas begin and end, where to pause, where to place emphasis, who is speaking, etc.
- *creative use* – to assist in conveying the tone of your

communication, to add humour and interest and increase the impact of your sentences

- *correct use* – to avoid misleading the reader or creating an impression of you and your company as unprofessional.

> A good way to test the effectiveness of punctuation is to read a sentence out loud; you will see quickly whether you are inserting pauses and emphasis in the right place.

11. The comma

Commas are a crucial form of punctuation, allowing you to extend the length and expand the content of a sentence. Commas are used mainly in the following ways:

- as a simple pause in a sentence (often doing the same job as 'and' or 'but')
- as a dividing mechanism, separating out a clause that relates to the main topic
- separating items in a list.

The following examples demonstrate the above points:

The company is planning expansion, building upon the successes of last year.
The company's planned expansion, announced earlier in the year, may affect local property values.
The planned expansion will entail growth in manufacturing, maintenance, warehousing and transportation.

Don't forget the second comma in a pair (as in the second example) and note that, in a list you should not place a comma after the penultimate item (as in the third example).

There is a common belief that you should never use a comma with 'and' or 'but'. Like most 'rules', this can be broken. The test should be whether the meaning is clear. Look at this example:

The planned expansion is likely to receive local support, and national backing too.

This sentence could be rewritten to avoid the 'problem', but it does work as above, with the comma aiding emphasis.

> Commas are crucial; a misplaced comma can seriously affect the meaning.

12. The semi-colon

Semi-colons are often considered to be 'more than a comma, less than a full stop'. Semi-colons mark a significant break in a sentence, usually dividing two separate, but related, ideas.

We have been exporting to the Far East for more than a decade; this year we expect Japan to be our largest overseas market.

In this example there is a clear link between the two parts. A pause created by a comma would probably be insufficient. A full stop might be too strong.

The managing director will be giving the keynote address;

she will be covering all the points discussed at the share-holders' meeting.

Here, the second part of the sentence would not work well on its own. The word 'she' is a pronoun, standing in place of a noun, in this case 'the managing director'. Linking the two elements using a semi-colon makes it immediately clear to whom the word 'she' refers.

Like any skill, your writing will improve with practice. This is especially true of forms of punctuation like the semi-colon, where there are no right and wrong uses – it is a matter of choice.

Semi-colons can sometimes be used to subdivide long lists in a sentence – but you will probably be better off using bullet point lists (see page 43):

Wright's subjects in this exhibition cover cities from three continents: Bombay, Calcutta and Bangkok; Berlin, Paris, Amsterdam and London; Chicago and New York; from Asia, Europe and North America respectively.

> Don't overuse any punctuation mark, especially not the semi-colon.

13. The colon

Colons signal that something different is about to follow. They are normally used before a list or quotation.

The roadshow will visit five British towns and cities: Oxford, Brighton, Liverpool, Newcastle and Oban.
When asked about the value of the roadshow, the Marketing

Manager, Bob Curran, had the following comments: "It's been exciting and exhausting, and worth every penny the company has spent."

Colons can also introduce displayed matter (outside the sentence) such as bullet point lists, indented quotes or equations and diagrams.

All cashiers are reminded of the difference between net and gross values:

net value + 17.5% (VAT) = gross value

A colon and a dash (:-) is hardly ever used in modern business communications. A colon does the job by itself. Note too that speech can be introduced with a comma instead of the colon.

> Consistency in using punctuation makes life easier for you and the reader.

14. Ending a sentence

It is important to let your reader know when a sentence has finished. This may sound like an obvious rule but it is often overlooked. The three most common ways are:

- full stop: usually placed at the completion of all other text and punctuation
- exclamation mark: should only be used very sparingly and probably never in formal business communications. They should appear at the end of sentences and do not need an accompanying full stop. Exclamation marks add

emphasis to statements: "The company's new product range is now on display. Don't miss it!"

- question mark: should come at the end of any sentence that includes a question, whether direct or rhetorical.

There was one question we all wanted to ask. What will the Chancellor do in the budget? Isn't about time the Chanceller thought about the plight of small businesses?

Sometimes a sentence might end with the full stop (exclamation mark or question mark) before inverted commas. The following is correct:

The Chancellor responded by saying: "There is nothing I'd like more than to give financial help to small firms, but it's not within my power at the present time."

> Full stops are vital signals to the reader. Don't forget them.

15. Parentheses

Items in parentheses are a separated part of a sentence. The separation is normally created by commas, dashes (see page 23) or brackets. When inserting words in parentheses it is important to ensure that the sentence still functions correctly without them. Commas, dashes and brackets work in different ways.

The C62 model, available in green and blue, will be released in February.
The C62 model – a mere 13 months from conception to completion – will be released in February.
The C62 model (the idea is the brainchild of Sir Samuel

McLeod who later went on to become head of engineering at CONCET) will be released in February.

In the first example the extra information is closely and directly related to the main information of the sentence, that 'The C62 model will be released in February.' In the second example the information in parentheses is linked, but stands alone – and stands out – much more distinctively. In the third example the information in parentheses is removed from the main point, but the writer still wishes to include it because it lends interest or colour. In every case the sentence still works without the text in parentheses.

Brackets are also useful for essential or interesting facts such as dates (born 1955), statistics (population 200,000) and explanations (excluding VAT).

> Don't overuse parentheses. Sometimes a separate sentence might be better.

16. The apostrophe

The apostrophe is one element of punctuation which can only be used either correctly or incorrectly; there is no room for creativity. Apostrophes are used to indicate:

- that a letter (or letters) have been omitted
- possession.

I'm sure that the sales team is wrong on this one, but they're a hard bunch to convince.
The Chief Executive's view is that the market will pick up; the directors' bonuses may be paid after all.

The above examples demonstrate the basic rules. Remember, there is just one Chief Executive (singular) so the word is followed by 's. There are several directors (plural) so the word is followed by just the apostrophe '; the s has been left off.

There are some other points to note:

- when a word in the singular ends in s (Harrods, Jones, etc.) then use just the apostrophe ' (Harrods', etc.) to show possession
- never use an apostrophe for the plural of numbers or initials (1960s, not 1960's and MPs, not MP's)
- it's means 'it is' or 'it has' and its means 'belonging to it'.

To confirm you have got it right:

An MP's car is one of the few perks that MPs receive. ✔
It's these MPs' cars that are in the way. ✔
Bishops' opinion of MPs has not changed since the '70s. ✔

> Incorrect use of any form of punctuation makes the writing look unprofessional.

17. The hyphen

The hyphen is not strictly a punctuation mark, but a means of making words more easy to read. Hyphens visibly link words that are bonded in their meaning. There are no hard and fast rules to govern the use of the hyphen, but below is a set of guidelines that will work for you every time.

Following these rules will ensure consistency and save you time:

- Use hyphens after prefixes such as neo-, sub-, quasi- etc, unless your dictionary shows them as joined. These prefixes do not make sense on their own.
- Use hyphens for words that need to be grouped together such as paint-by-numbers, 18-year-old, state-of-the-art when they relate to another word (eg. 18-year-old car, state-of-the-art computer, etc.).
- Use hyphens for describing words that are linked in their meaning such as wholly-owned, project-based, exchange-listed etc, when these relate to another word (eg. wholly-owned subsidiary or project-based example).
- Do *not* use hyphens for simple pairings of adjectives and nouns such as Chief Executive, primary industry, client server, etc., or for linking two describing words such as totally different, vastly expensive, etc.

This example may help you understand the difference between the last two points.

The second-hand computer was user friendly. ✔
The user-friendly computer was second hand. ✔

> Most 'rules' are there to help you; they promote consistency and aid understanding. Remember, however, that the main aim is to communicate successfully. This should guide your decisions.

18. Inverted commas (quotation marks)

In writing we can use either single or double inverted commas (or quotation marks).

Double inverted commas are mostly used for direct speech:

"We must create a bigger impact," he explained, "in both home and overseas markets."

Single inverted commas have a variety of uses:

- reported speech: *The focus group was said to have produced the 'best ever' set of results.*
- words that are being used (deliberately) in a different context from normal: *We consider it best that this idea is 'put on ice' until market conditions change.*
- specialist words introduced for the first time: *We will reproduce some of the illustrations as 'duotones' to create the right effect.*
- to suggest irony or a pun: *The union had some views concerning the management's 'commitment' to equal pay.*

> With the wide availability of word processors the use of italic fonts has replaced many instances where single inverted commas may formerly have been used. These include the names of works of art such as film and book titles, newspaper names and foreign language terms.

19. Other punctuation marks

There are several other punctuation marks that you can use to add greater clarity and interest to your writing.

Dashes

Dashes are longer than hyphens. Dashes separate words and hyphens pull words together. Dashes should strictly be called 'en-dashes' as they are the width of the 'n' character. They are normally the key strokes option + hyphen or created by alt + hyphen. Dashes can be used in pairs to separate out items in parentheses (see page 18) or singly to pull out a phrase that requires emphasis:

The exceptionally quiet spell in August meant that sales were well down – by 20 per cent overall.

Ellipsis

An ellipsis is the three dots that can be used to add an afterthought to a sentence.

Sales were well down on last year, with a 20 per cent drop in some cases … and it could have been a lot worse.

There is little difference between the dash and ellipsis in the above examples. Use the dash where you wish to make an impact and the ellipsis for adding less vital pieces of information. Note also that ellipsis is also used to indicate that words have been deliberately omitted from a quote:

'This has been a great year … the best on record.'

Full points

Full points often cause confusion. Your company may have a house style that you have to follow, or you may have a way of working that suits you. If you are in doubt, here is a rule that will work every time:

- Do not use full points for capital letter abbreviations such as NATO, UNESCO, MP, BT, VAT, etc.
- Use full points at the end of abbreviations that end in a lower case character such as eg., ie., etc., Dr., Prof., etc. (except when following numbers such as 22km, 100 ha, 50th, 42nd, etc.).

Remember to address people as they have addressed themselves. If they write F.R.S. or Mr, it is polite to reply with similar punctuation.

20. Numbers in your text

You will often need to use numbers in the course of your business writing. As always, the key is to be consistent. Ideally your company will have a house style that will stop you having to make a separate decision on every occasion. In the absence of a house style, here are some rules that may help:

- spell out 'one' to 'ten' (four people, six times, etc.) unless linked to units (8kg, 2ha, etc.)
- use numerals for almost everything else (88 cars, 120 votes), but use words for generalisations ('fifty or so', 'thousands of times' and 'over a hundred', etc.)
- do not start sentences with numerals
- use lower case for units when with numerals (22km, 110ha, 100g, etc.)
- fractions (if not too many of them) are often better spelt out (three-quarters, one-third, etc.)

- dates are best expressed as 3 February 1997
- do not use commas up to 9999. Thereafter, use them (12,886, 122,743, etc.).

This list doesn't cover everything. Remember too that you will need to make exceptions to these rules from time to time. Always try to be consistent, and always keep the reader in mind.

21. Editing your work

Writing in a simple and effective fashion and punctuating creatively and correctly are major steps towards good business writing. There are, however, a number of other factors to consider before documents can be released to your colleagues or customers. You should edit your work carefully to ensure that you have:

- avoided basic grammatical pitfalls
- eliminated spelling errors
- cut to a length that you think is appropriate
- guaranteed that the meaning is clear.

Why are these points so important? Grammatical and spelling errors will make the writing look unprofessional, reflecting badly on you and your company. In extreme situations, errors may change the meaning. The extent of a document is vital too. In business there is often very little time to read things carefully. In long documents key points may be overlooked completely. Finally, you need always to ensure that the reader understands exactly what you mean.

It is easy to have a clear idea in your mind but end up with a muddled explanation on the page.

These points are covered in the next few pages.

> If you follow the basic rules, editing time will be cut down.

22. Sentence structure and order

We have already looked at the rules for constructing successful basic sentences (page 8). As you build longer sentences, however, you will find problems arising. As you construct a sentence, think about its shape and structure. Is it easy to follow? Are you 'tripping up' the reader?

Do not always write as you think

One of the reasons why sentences become muddled is because we sometimes write as we think. For example:

You have been asked to attend, the exact date has yet to be fixed, a preliminary hearing before 10 May 1998.

The writer suddenly remembered that the 'exact date' was not fixed and inserted that fact as she remembered it. A more logical, and easier to understand, sequence might have been:

You have been asked to attend a preliminary hearing before 10 May 1998; the exact date has yet to be fixed.

Always think about the logic and flow of the sentence from the reader's viewpoint. Do not rely upon your own first instincts.

Use familiar and consistent patterns

Here is an example of a sentence that might cause difficulty:

The management of the company relies heavily upon both excellent training and not having a problem of absenteeism.

The construction 'both ... and' will be familiar. The reader, however, will expect the two items listed to be similar. The first, 'excellent training', is positive and succinct. The second, 'not having a problem of absenteeism', is partly negative and quite wordy. This clumsy construction may confuse the reader.

Here is another example:

Successful companies are usually well managed, highly motivated and they possess a sense of drive.

The meaning is relatively clear but the reader will be tripped up by the structure. The sentence begins as if it is going to use a common structure, that of three items in a short list. The first two items, 'well managed' and 'highly motivated', are simple adverbial phrases. The third, 'they possess a sense of drive', is a separate clause with its own verb. This may cause the reader to stumble. It might have been better to write 'very dynamic' or 'strongly proactive' instead.

Check the word order

It is very easy to get words in the wrong order without noticing it. Look at this example:

The instructions not only stress regular maintenance by the operator but also annual inspection by the manufacturers.

The sentence uses the familiar construction 'not only ... but also'. The writer intends to balance 'regular maintenance' and 'annual inspection'. Unfortunately, the words 'not only' are placed before 'stress'; they should be before 'regular maintenance'.

Check your clarity

This is not a 'rule' of grammar, just a reminder to you to check that you make your meaning very clear. This sentence shows a typical problem:

I attended a meeting with some colleagues in the sales department.

Was the meeting 'in the sales department' or was the meeting with some colleagues 'from' the sales department? Ensure your meaning is clear.

Here is another area where confusion may occur:

Writing courses can be very tedious.

Does the writer mean writing courses that you can attend, or the process of writing courses? The sentence is ambiguous. Always take a moment to reread your work to ensure you avoid simple errors like these.

> Writing 'as we speak' can create fresh, simple communications – but always check that your meaning is clear.

23. Using pronouns carefully

Pronouns are words that stand in the place of nouns. We regularly use several types, some of which include:

- personal pronouns – I, we, you, they, etc.

- relative pronouns – who, whose, that, which, etc.
- demonstrative pronouns – that, this, those, these, etc.
- indefinite – any, each, several, some, etc. (ie I have *several*, you don't have *any*.)

We use pronouns all the time and could not write without them. The important point is to ensure that the reader knows to what you are referring when you use a pronoun. Look at these examples:

The company sponsor the local basketball team. It *has just had a brilliant year.*
Imports and exports are affected by the recession; both *have decreased.*

In the first example the pronoun 'it' could refer to either the company or the team. It is not clear to the reader which is intended. In the second example, 'both' is the pronoun. The reader will understand that 'both' refers to 'Imports and exports' because the word 'both' implies a pair.

Imports and exports are affected by inflation and recession; both will decrease.

By contrast, in this example there is considerable confusion about what 'both' refers to. It is your job to make everything clear.

> The message is that pronouns are valuable words that we cannot do without – but you must take care when you use them.

24. Check your verbs

Verbs are the 'doing' words in a sentence. When editing your work you should check:

- the tense
- the agreement.

Tense

In long sentences and paragraphs there is a danger of changing tense:

The wage freeze had affected productivity. Staff will be demotivated; they have noticed the effect on their pay packets immediately the New Year started.

This will give the reader a confused sense of time. Is the pay-freeze still active? Are the staff demotivated already or will they be when they see their pay packets? Clearly, the above is example is rather extreme, but more subtle errors often occur:

The staff have been demotivated when they saw their pay awards.

Agreement

Make sure your verb agrees with the noun that defines it (the subject).

The company knows the value of its sales team and have appointed two new representatives.

This is incorrect because the company is singular and (it) 'knows the value'. Later the writer makes the company plural when he says (they) 'have appointed two new representatives'.

Remember, collective nouns (words that represent a collection of individual items) are usually singular, eg. government, team, cabinet, company, etc.

> Except in special circumstances, every sentence should contain an active verb.

25. Choice of words

Check that your writing is crisp and free of cliché, jargon and redundant words.

Cliché

Clichés are words or phrases that are used too often and, as a result, lose both meaning and impact. Here are some clichés popular at the time of writing (bear in mind that fashions change over time):

with the current state of the economy
a major new (series, concept, production, etc.)
teetering on the brink
at the end of the day

Jargon

Jargon is a language used within a particular group of people and not necessarily understood beyond that group. Therefore you must be aware of your readers. Look at this example:

The process of upskilling will be completed once the course has been run.

'Upskilling' is used within the world of human resources,

where it has a specific meaning. Beyond this group, however, the word will be largely unfamiliar.

Redundant words

Avoid redundant words in your writing. We may get away with them in everyday speech but they take valuable time to write and read. Look at these examples:

> *first and foremost = first*
> *as and when = when*
> *general consensus of opinion = consensus*

If you were to say 'first, and foremost,' the commas would emphasise the words 'and foremost', creating impact. 'First and foremost' without punctuation is very limp.

> We constantly alter the way we use language, so what is jargon, slang or considered ungrammatical today may be acceptable in the future.

26. Cutting the extent

There is rarely time, in business, to read carefully and systematically. Most people skim through documents, no matter how important they are. For this reason it is important that you keep your writing to the necessary minimum. Each extra and unnecessary word detracts from the value of the important and essential words. Word processors make cutting a relatively painless task – unlike the days of typewriters and correcting fluid!

You have already been urged to use simple words (page 8) and to cut out redundant words (page 32). Both these strategies will help you write tightly. Now think about further pruning of your work.

Meaningless descriptions

In speech we are apt to use words that have very little meaning. They take little time to say and get lost in the general interchange of conversation. Written words, however, carry more weight. You should try to cut these valueless words out unless you really mean them.

The meeting is very important.
We will hear if they have any doubts.
The market varies considerably from this time last year.

In each case the use of the descriptive words (adjectives and adverbs) may have value, but probably not. You must decide; try to derive maximum benefit from what few descriptive words you use.

Words and phrases that add nothing

Apart from descriptors we use other words and phrases that add no meaning – only clutter – to sentences. Look at these examples. Imagine the sentences without the underlined words:

This letter is by way of informing you that the management committee decided to implement all the recommendations of the Smith Report 1997.
We are in the process of reviewing our production strategy.
Money is required to be invested in the development of the German plant.
Please note that the cheque was sent to you on 23 March.

You will have to decide how cutting affects the tone of your document. You may wish to include one or two phrases that the reader will consider to be polite. As a general rule, however, your readers will appreciate short and succinct communications that get straight to the point.

Repeated words and phrases

As you build longer documents you will find you are referring to the same facts or concepts repeatedly. This is unavoidable, but make sure you do not repeat unnecessary words.

For example, you may begin writing about a conference held 'in the Scottish town, Kinross'. After the first mention of 'in the Scottish town' you can just say 'Kinross'. You may write about 'work about to be carried out in the autumn'. After the first mention, you can call this 'the work'.

It is hard to illustrate this point more fully without long examples. Be aware of the problem. If you need help use the search function on your word processor to highlight repetition; you can then decide whether it is essential or not.

Rereading – and rewriting

The above ideas will help you make quick changes to your work in order to reduce the extent. Sometimes you will find that sentences are overlong but can only be shortened by thorough rewriting. It is up to you to decide how much time you have for this process. Here are just two examples to indicate the kinds of change that can be made:

The committee, having looked objectively at the process of reordering, took the decision that the time was not right, because of the present despatch procedures, to completely revamp the process. ✗
The committee considered the reordering process and decided that the existing despatch procedures militated against change. ✓
In the event of a court summons the company will have to

present all relevant materials to the magistrate in order that he or she can pronounce whether the case should go to a higher court or be heard in the magistrate's court. ✘
Following a summons the magistrate will decide, based upon the materials supplied by the company, where the case will be heard. ✔

Remember, there are few right and wrong decisions in the matter of cutting; you have decide what is relevant and appropriate.

> Short sentences – ideally fewer than 20 words – are essential for good business writing.

27. Measuring readability

There are two relatively well-known methods for assessing the readability of your work – or the work of others. These are outlined below. You should use these formulae only rarely, if at all. They might be valuable if you wish to measure improvement in writing over time, or the success of an editing stage. Note that both formulae use sentence length (keep them short) and word length (keep them short) as determining factors.

The tests you can apply are:

Reading ease test (developed by Rudolph Flesch in the 1940s)

Step 1	Average sentence length × 1.015 = A
Step 2	Number of syllables per 100 words × 0.846 = B
Step 3	Add two (A+B) together = C
Step 4	Subtract answer (C) from 206.8 = readability
Note	0 = unreadable > > > 100 = very readable

Fog index (developed by Robert Gunning in the 1960s)

Step 1 Average sentence length = A
Step 2 Percentage of words with three syllables or more = B
Step 3 Add two (A+B) together = C
Step 4 Multiply C × 0.4 = fog index
Note 0 = very readable > > > 10 = becoming hard > > > 20 = very hard

28. Proof reading

Careful reading of any document is the best way to create a professional image. Although small grammatical errors may not change the meaning, they will reflect badly on the writer. Here are a few tips that will improve your proof reading:

- If the document is very important, ask colleagues to check it for you. You are more likely to miss things in your own writing.
- Do not rely solely on the spell checker on your word processor. They will not highlight alternative spellings (eg. you for your, there for their, etc.).
- Focusing upon the detail of a document such as amounts, values, foreign spellings, etc., may cause you to miss more obvious errors in the remainder of your work.
- Above all, check the spelling of names (especially customers' names) as errors here can cause offence and embarrassment, especially if you have received a correctly spelt communication from them.

A quiet room and undivided attention to the task regularly produce the best results, although there is no way of guaranteeing 100 per cent accuracy every time. There is, however, a technique that usually picks up *all* the small errors. If you have time, read your document backwards, from the last word to the first. This method ensures that you pay attention to every individual word and do not skim read.

> With all editing and proof reading you are balancing time spent against value added. It is your choice.

29. Clear meaning

The last point about editing might be the most important. You should always ensure that the meaning of your text is clear. This means checking not only the general sense of the words, but also the emphasis and tone. It is very easy to write something that sounds fine in your own head, but which is unclear to the reader. We become so used to our own writing style that we often forget other people may have trouble understanding it.

There is no simple solution to achieving clear meaning. The best advice is to give your document a 'fresh' read. This means either:

- asking a colleague to read the document for you, or
- reading it again yourself after a break from writing.

A good tip is to read out loud, ensuring that you do not stumble over the construction and that the emphasis is clearly defined by the punctuation. Remember, even the most experienced practitioners rarely get it right first time, so don't skimp on the time spent checking.

Going back over work can be a time-consuming chore – but the benefits are likely to outweigh the costs.

30. The professional document

No matter how good your text is, it will have no value if it remains unread. You must ensure that every document is well organised and well set out. It must be accessible to your reader. The following pages look at the skills required to ensure a professional finish to your work. In particular you should consider the following points:

- **consistency and agreement** – have you used the same styles and spellings throughout, are the headings and contents the same, are page references correct?
- **organisation** – is the document well planned, is the structure obvious, can the reader find their way around?
- **headings** – do they add value and/or interest, are they good signposts for your document?
- **lists** – are they clear and consistent, do they follow the basic rules?
- **layout** - is it clear, have you used the word processor effectively, have you overused the word processor?

Take into account the span of people's attention. You must make your documents easy to read.

31. Consistency and agreement

Consistency in written work is important. It makes the difference between a professional and unprofessional document. The following sections outline a number of areas to consider.

Many companies provide a 'house style' which makes decisions for you. If you do not follow a house style you may find the best policy is to buy a guide to English usage which you can use as a handy reference book. *Hart's Rules,* published by Oxford University Press, is recommended. You need to achieve consistency in two areas:

Use of words and punctuation

Think carefully about the following:

- *hyphens* – see page 20
- *capitalisation* – when presented with a choice, lower case is preferable.

The following examples illustrate good practice; but also some of the problems of trying to be consistent.

The Managing Director approached the Maybury District Council for their opinion regarding the 1989 Act. ✔
Managing directors often use district councils as scapegoats when finding their plans blocked by Acts of Parliament. ✔

In the second example you may have thought that Acts of Parliament should have been lower case, but since it means *the* UK Parliament you should use an initial capital for Parliament. The phrase 'acts of Parliament' may trip up the reader; 'Acts of Parliament' looks much better.

- *spelling* – you will have to make a choice where alternative spellings exist. Remember that British spelling normally uses -ise- in words like realise, standardise, etc.

- *numbers* – see page 24.
- *abbreviations* – see page 23.

Internal structure

- *agreement of tense, subject, etc.* – follow your choices through. For example, if you start a letter saying 'we', don't switch to 'I'
- *contents and headings* – make sure there is agreement throughout the document.

If you introduce a topic with (a), (b) and (c) as headings, don't switch to 1, 2 and 3. If you use 1, 2 and 3, don't switch to 1., 2. and 3. Do all your headings use initial capitals? Have you used 'and' in one heading and '&' in another? Does your contents list correspond with your headings?

Being consistent not only makes life easier for your reader but will help you too. Once you have established a style you will not have to make individual decisions – just follow the 'rules' you have set yourself.

> A company house style decreases time spent on decision making and increases the level of professionalism in documents.

32. Organisation

All documents, from short letters to extensive reports, need a clear structure. This will help readers find their way around the text. Headings are the most common way of breaking up text and providing signposts. They should be planned with a hierarchy in mind. It is convenient to use letters to aid planning (see below). Look at these examples of headings taken from a 80-page report on employment.

Try either:

3 Policy into practice

3.1 To declare or not to declare

3.2 Application forms

3.2.1 Finding out about disability

3.2.1.1 Strengths and weaknesses

3.2.2 Health and disability

or

Policy into practice

To declare or not to declare

Application forms

Finding out about disability

Strengths and weaknesses

Health and disability

The first example uses a numbering system which aids cross referencing. You can of course use a mixture of numbers and letters: 3 followed by A B C, perhaps followed by i ii iii. The second example has the same hierarchy but uses changes in style to indicate the relative weight of each heading. This helps a document look attractive. Note that the changes are all variations of the same font (larger size, bold, italic, etc.); this gives a cleaner look than using different fonts.

Before deciding on headings, think about how the document is going to be used. Then remember to keep the structure simple and consistent.

There are a few other points of organisation that should be considered:

- *page numbers* – word processors can add these automatically
- *cross-references* – these are useful (sometimes essential), but try to keep them to a minimum
- *an index* – might be helpful in a larger document
- *footnotes* – can be difficult to organise, but may be more useful to a reader than notes at the end of a document
- *running heads and feet* – provide a quick visual reminder of position
- *glossaries, appendices, lists of illustrations, etc.* – all these items (and others) may be helpful, but always try to simplify; do not make your reader flip from place to place.

> You can use headings in letters if this aids communication.

33. Lists

Lists help break down information into easy-to-read units.

Bullet point lists

These are ideal where there is a small amount of information to be contained in each point. To be consistent, try to:

- use a colon as the punctuation before the list
- use lower case and not capitals to commence each point*
- avoid repetition at the start of each point
- keep the structure consistent for each point
- punctuate (with a full stop) the last point only.*

Don't forget that you are not restricted to using bullets. Word processors provide plenty of options such as boxes, arrows, pointing fingers, etc.

Numbered lists

These should be used when you wish to make reference to the information elsewhere. Keep the numbering simple and consistent. For example, use numbers 1, 2, 3 etc. You do not need to use full points, brackets, underlining or other devices.

If you have sub-lists, try using (a), (b) or (i), (ii) etc. Brackets are useful here, as lower case letters do not stand out so well when in isolation.

Indenting the information, or separating it with a line

* Where complete sentences are being used in each unit you should use full stops at the end of each item.

space are other means of adding clarity. Above all, consistency is important. Ensure that each list is set out in the same way.

> Remember, being bulleted rather than numbered means that the items are not so rigidly ranked.

34. Layout

The layout of documents has been revolutionised by the development of word processing: but try not to be too ambitious. The best layouts are the most simple. Remember, clarity is the key for textual documents.

Where you want to integrate text and illustrations, or to create design impact (eg. in an advertisement or display) the best advice is to use an expert – work with a trained designer.

For straightforward documents:

- Use as few fonts as possible. Ideally stick to one, using different sizes and styles (ie. bold, italic, etc.).
- Choose a standard font that is easy to read, not a 'special' font designed for display purposes.
- Do not make your line length too long; the longer the line, the harder it will be to read.
- Keep special characteristics such as underlining, indentations, etc. to a consistent and workable minimum. Use justified setting only rarely as it can create awkward word spacing.
- Check the head and foot of pages. Wherever possible,

headings should not fall at the foot, lists should not be split (like this one!), etc.

- Think about line spacing. You may wish to leave more than single line spacing in certain situations.
- Try to avoid 'widows' – individual words left alone at the tops of pages or the end of paragraphs.

> The word processor provides a great opportunity to create consistent styles. Storing templates for letters, tenders, memos, etc., will save a lot of time.

35. Developing your skills further

Creating effective and professional documents should be your first target. Accuracy, conciseness and consistency will combine to produce professional communications.

Beyond these basics, however, are questions of style and tone. Is your writing interesting as well as informative? Are you conveying the right level of friendliness or formality? Will people be drawn into your document, or will they be put off? We will consider these issues over the next few pages. In particular you should consider:

- The recipient – what are the readers' expectations or prejudices?; what will please or offend them?
- The impression – what tone do you wish to create: friendly, formal, grateful, angry, etc.?
- The effect – are you trying to influence or persuade somebody? (See page 6 for information on writing for effect.)

- The need to read – will this document be read anyway, or do I have to grab the reader's attention?

> With spoken communications you can always explain or backtrack; with written communications you often have just one shot at creating the right impression.

36. What do you want to achieve?

When you think about writing, especially letters which are direct personal communications, consider both your aims and the expectations of your reader. Your choice of words is vital. Consider the difference between these words:

client	*customer*
portfolio	*list*
team	*staff*
affordable	*cheap*
creating	*making*

These pairs of words have approximately the same meaning, but create very different impressions. There are no right or wrong answers, but you must be aware of your aims and your customer's (or client's!) expectations.

Think about these words:

problems

concerns

anxieties

worries

These can be described as negative words. You could choose a more neutral word: try *issues.* Your choice of words will influence the tone and perhaps the design of letters and other documents. As mentioned above, you should consider:

- *Your aims* – what relationship do you wish to have with the recipient?; what result do you wish your letter to achieve?
- *Your reader's needs* – could your letter cause offence – or bring pleasure? Is the reader a traditionalist. Is English their first language?

Note some of the ways in which you can set the tone of a letter. Are you going to write 'The Company', 'we' or 'I'? Consider the different impact of these endings to letters:

Yours sincerely

Kind regards

Best wishes

Getting the reaction you want also depends on your choice of phrases. Think about the following. How would your reader respond to each?

Please can you send the information as soon as possible.

Please send the information as soon as possible.

Send the information as soon as possible.

The difference in tone can easily be detected.

The above sentences raise another important issue. What response is the phrase 'as soon as possible' likely to elicit? Would it be better saying 'by March 4th', for example?

Think about the 'throwaway' phrases we all use from time to time. Do the following have any impact, or could other, more specific, phrases be used instead?

the document is sent _for your information_
the _copy*_ is sent _for your attention_
please return it _without further delay_
the committee thought the proposal was _very interesting_

Your choice of words is vital.

Remember also that you will create the wrong impression if you write to a fastidious customer in an informal manner, or use Eurocentric cultural references in a letter to a Japanese client. Remember also that if a person signs himself in a formal way, adding letters after his name, this is probably the way he or she would like to addressed.

> There is much to be said on this topic but little hard advice that is possible. The best advice is probably be aware, be flexible and (ultimately) be yourself.

37. Pulling your readers in

Much of the advice in this book is given assuming that readers will *have* to take notice of what you write. This is not always the case. Often you will be competing for the attention of your reader.

Assuming you have already followed the basic advice – making your documents clear and concise – what else can you do to grab, and hold, your reader's attention?

How people read

How do you read? Do you often turn the pages from the

* Is it a copy, or is it just another original run off the same word processor's memory?

back of a document first? Do you look at the illustrations before the text? Do you skim read, or follow every word methodically? With longer documents you may be tempted to spend most time on the core text, but this will probably be what the reader looks at last. It is more likely that the reader will notice:

- *headings* – main and subheadings, which are in large type and easy to spot
- *captions* – these will be short and accompany (interesting) illustrations
- *quotes* – we all love 'sound bites'
- *sidebars and other words* – key words and phrases that can appear on pages to send a quick message
- *highlighted words and phrases* – such as key terms in bold, etc.

Headings

Try to use headings effectively, as:

- *guides* to your reader, indicating what is in each section of your document
- *attention grabbers*, surprising or amusing your reader
- *teasers*, inviting the reader to find out more.

You can also use your headings to tell a story of their own so that the reader can get an impression of the contents without having to read the whole text.

The first few words

If your reader has decided to dip into your text he or she will be influenced by the first few words, so these deserve special attention. Consider the impact of these opening sentences, all concerning the same topic:

You may wish to think about your own liability in the event of a death at your workplace.
Do you know your legal position if somebody dies in the workplace?
Death! It could be you.

While not suggesting that any of these are the perfect solution, they do demonstrate different approaches. The first personalises the issue, the second asks a leading question (inviting you to read on to find out) while the third causes surprise and – hopefully – inquisitiveness.

> Effective communications need not lack colour; they can be interesting, challenging and amusing.

38. Adding style

You can employ a range of techniques to add a touch of style to your documents. Always remember, do not:

- obscure the message
- overuse any one technique
- forget your reader.

Below are just four of the many techniques that can be used.

Alliteration

Strictly, alliteration means the repeated use of the same initial sound in a sequence of words.

Writing that uses alliterative style can be imaginative, impressive and impactful.

However, you can stretch this definition and use words that simply sound good together. For example:

If alliteration is used in a clear, crisp and concise way, the writing can be very effective.
For greater effect, but for writing that is still pertinent and practical, there is no need to stick to the basic rules.

The key is to try to make the writing as easy to read as possible. Try reading your sentences out loud to see if the text flows well. Small improvements can make all the difference.

Creative punctuation

We have already looked at using punctuation to aid understanding (pages 13-24), but it can also be used to make your writing more interesting and more memorable.

Written communications – from formal letters to hurried faxes and e-mail notes – are more important than ever before.
Although spoken communications are easier than ever we can never dispense with the written word... passionate, powerful and permanent.
The pen? Mightier than the sword!

Metaphor

You probably use metaphor more than you think. It is the description of one object or idea in terms of another. Look at these examples:

The factory is operating at full throttle.
The company scored a classic own goal when it missed the deadline for tax returns.

In the first case the writer is comparing the factory with a car; in the second case a sporting metaphor is used.

The keys to successful use of metaphor are:

- follow a metaphor throughout a document, building a framework
- don't overuse any metaphor – keep it subtle
- don't mix metaphors within the document.

Popular metaphors such as those associated with sport or travel will help a reader feel comfortable with the writing while adding a little colour and interest.

Adjectival power

When you wish to describe a new product or idea you will want to use positive adjectives. Look at these examples:

> *The Omega Mark II is the latest addition to the range; it is stylishly designed and ready for the shops*
> *The stylishly designed Omega Mark II, the latest addition to the range, is ready for the shops*
> *This stylishly designed latest addition to the range is ready for the shops*

The meaning is the same in each case, but the tone (and the length) is different. In the first example the facts are simply stated. In the second example the words 'stylishly designed' are attached to the name of the product, forming an association in the reader's mind. In the third example the writer has omitted the name of the product altogether – a technique that may be valuable if you wish to avoid repetition of the product's name.

Remember how people read documents – often by skim reading. By having a range of relevant descriptions scattered through the document you will create an overall impression, rather than simply making a number of separate points.

> Think how far your own skills will stretch before you need to use a specialist copywriter. You may be surprised how much value a copywriter can add to your brief.

39. Breaking the rules

If you make a mistake in writing you will 'trip up' the reader. Sometimes you may want to do this intentionally. This is best attempted once you are confident about your writing skills.

Consider these sentences (or in the first case, a non-sentence):

> *High Tech; Engineering/Manufacturing; Financial Services; Retail; Leisure. We have clients in all these areas of commercial activity.*
>
> *The company has been affected by the trials and tribulations of establishing an Asian sales network. Easy it was not.*
>
> *The turns, trials, tribulations of working in Asia may cause a few grumbles, but the rewards are immense.*

In the first case the writer has simply inserted a list. It is not a sentence, but it works well and sends an immediate signal to the reader. If you're in the list, then read on. If you're not in the list, perhaps this article is not for you.

In the second case the writer wishes to make one point

clear: that it's not easy working in Asia. To make sure that the reader notices the point he makes it with a rather odd sentence construction. The reader is more likely to remember this than some other, more formal, sentence.

In the third example the writer has omitted the word 'and' from the threesome 'turns, trials, tribulations'. He or she probably wishes the reader to consider all three words as being of equal importance. Had the phrase 'turns, trials *and* tribulations' been used, the reader may have considered 'and tribulations' to be less important. Try saying the two phrases out loud to emphasise this point.

In each of three cases the writer has done something out of the ordinary in order to trip up the readers and gain their attention.

> Remember, you can only start breaking the rules when you are fully in command of the basic skills.

40. Using your new skills

The actual skills of business writing – using punctuation creatively, influencing your reader, proof reading accurately, etc. – will help you prepare professional documents. These key skills, however, need to be supported by others. For example, you should also consider:

- how you prepare to write – document planning
- how to get started – avoiding 'writer's block'
- timing and scheduling
- choosing your tools – what hardware and software

- working with others - various models for collaborative writing.

Look at how others write, how punctuation is used, what vocabulary is employed. Learning from the strengths – and weaknesses – of others is a fruitful way to improve your own skills.

41. Preparing to write

Although word processors make editing easy, it is still a good idea to plan a document, especially a long report or letter, before beginning to write. A plan will ensure a better organised document and less time wasted on revisions.

Planning need not take a great deal of time. Simply jot a few headings down to remind yourself of the key points you wish to cover. Remember to organise the hierarchy of headings too (see page 41).

Mind Mapping®

One good way of planning your writing is to modify a technique called Mind Mapping®.

1. In the centre of a large piece of paper, write the name of your topic.
2. Around the paper, in any position, note down all the related points you may wish to make.
3. When you have exhausted everything you can think of, start linking up the various points into groups (which may become chapters or paragraphs).
4. Once the points are linked up (and you may choose to exclude some) you can number them a paragraphs or sections of your document.

The advantages of Mind Mapping® which may be best tackled collaboratively, include:

- you can enlist the help of others in initial planning
- you move quickly from a 'jumble' of ideas to a well ordered diagram
- you can plan visually, which some people prefer
- your completed chart acts as a checklist when you have finished your writing.

42. Getting started

Often it is hard to get started with a writing project. We put it off until the last minute. Here are four techniques that may help.

Divert your attention

Once you have the brief in your mind, walk away from the task for a short while. You may, consciously, be involved in some other task but your brain will be working away on the brief. When you rejoin the job you will be refreshed and, hopefully, ready to begin.

Notebook in advance

You can be sure that you will think of a perfect phrase or a catchy slogan when you are least expecting it. If you can make a note of your thoughts at the time you will not only remember them but have something to start with when you do begin writing.

Speak your thoughts

The words we write are only extensions of the thoughts we have. A good way to get started is to talk out loud; express your thoughts in the simplest way possible, with speech. Then write down your thoughts and begin to work them into sentences.

Get something down

Often we are slow to begin a task because there is resistance to the process of writing. Try to overcome this by beginning the physical process. Type anything: restate the brief, perhaps; or simply begin with some key words. Type out names and addresses. Key in the paragraph plan. With a word processor it is easy to edit and delete, so it doesn't matter how many of your original words are actually used.

> Balancing your writing time with physical exercise will often stimulate creativity.

43. You're not alone

There is a belief that writing is something that can only be done alone – perhaps in a garret! This need not be the case.

Help with the writing process

There are several ways you might choose to work with others.

The classic manager/assistant model

When you (the assistant) are asked to write something that somebody else (the manager) is going to approve, remember the following:

- Ask for a detailed brief – has the manager really thought it through? Can you help with this?

- Ensure you agree on the basics – what are the contents, who will read it, why are you writing it?
- Insist on a debriefing – why are changes being made, what is wrong (or right) with the first draft?

A lot of time can be wasted when the assistant prepares a good first draft only to have it largely rewritten by the manager. Remember this danger, whether you are in the role of the assistant or the manager.

The co-operative model

If you work with a colleague you can bounce ideas off each other, combine the strengths of your separate styles and double the likelihood of spotting errors of content or tone. However, there are some possible pitfalls:

- by trying to co-operate successfully with your colleague you may hide your true views about a piece of work
- text can become bland by conforming to a lowest common denominator
- the time spent by two individuals may not prove to be cost-effective.

Using others as a resource

In many areas of work, you take sole responsibility for what you do. Ultimately, this will be the case with documents that bear your name. However, you can try to increase your chances of success and minimise the risk of failure by asking others for help. Colleagues may be able to:

- tell you whether the meaning is immediately clear
- spot simple grammatical errors
- give their views on content, tone and style.

Think carefully about time constraints and the importance of a document, then decide who you can ask. Don't forget that if you ask somebody for an opinion you will receive one – but remember, you don't have to act upon it.

The keys to working with others are:

- ask them to become involved at an early stage; their input could help form strategies for later time/money saving
- be flexible in your approach and allow the design and illustrative considerations to be matched with your copy
- keep the final user in mind, ensuring that their needs/expectations are being met.

> Remember, the needs of the reader should always be uppermost in your mind.

44. Parts of speech – checklist

Business writing is all about communication. You do not need to know all the names of parts of speech to be able to write successfully. The following list, however, provides a very quick checklist which may help you appreciate the rules you are (inadvertently?) following and understand references to parts of speech made in this book and elsewhere.

Nouns

Nouns are naming words:

- *common nouns:* paper, pen, pork, picnic
- *proper nouns:* Manchester, Margaret, Monday

- *collective nouns:* team, troupe, government, group
- *abstract nouns:* happiness, horror, humour, honesty.

Pronouns

Pronouns are words used in the place of nouns:

- *personal* (in the place of a personal name or names): I, you, me, them, my
- *reflexive* (referring back to a person or persons): yourself, himself, themselves, myself
- *relative* (relating a noun to something else): whose, which, that, whom
- *interrogative* (asking a question about a noun): which, whose, what, whom
- *demonstrative* (referring clearly to an unstated noun): these, those, this, that
- *indefinite* (referring collectively to an unstated noun): several, any, each.

Verbs

Verbs are doing words. They may be:

- *transitive* (the action transfers from the subject to the object): John is hitting Gill; John knows Gill; John misunderstood Gill
- *intransitive* (where no action takes place): John laughs a lot; Gill feels ill

Verbs have a tense. The main types are:

- *present:* John is happy; Gill hears a cry
- *past:* John was happy; Gill heard a cry

- *future:* John will be happy; Gill will hear a cry.

Verbs can also be described as active or passive:

- *active* (where the subject of the sentence performs the action): John eats the dinner; Gill knows the score
- *passive* (where the subject of the sentence is on the receiving end of the action): the dinner was eaten by John; the score was known to Gill.

Adjectives

Adjectives describe nouns:

- *positive:* John is a brilliant golfer; Gill drives a green car
- *comparative:* John is a better golfer than Gill; Gill could not want a nicer meal
- *superlative:* John is the best golfer; Gill ate the biggest cake.

Adverbs

Adverbs qualify other words:

- *verbs:* John is singing beautifully; the case is firmly closed
- *adjectives:* John is a very famous politician; the man is only just alive.

Prepositions

Prepositions tell us more about verbs:

- John competed <u>for</u> the trophy; Gill jumped <u>into</u> the pool.

Conjunctions

Conjunctions join parts of a sentence: but, and, because, before, when, etc.

Subject and object

- the *subject* is the part of the sentence that performs the main action: John hits the ball; Gill drives a big car
- the *object* is on the receiving end of the action: John hits the ball; Gill drives a big car.

> Understanding grammar is not essential but it helps you to spot where and how you can go wrong.

45. Five-point reminders

This book is all about skills – skills you can apply to any type of business writing. Your thinking, however, should be driven by the specified type of work you are tackling. Below are five-point reminders of the skills to consider when tackling each of the most common types of writing – letters, reports and electronic communications (faxes and e-mails):

Letters

- Are you following house style?
- Is the titling correct?
- Is the tone appropriate?
- Do you want a response, and if so, will your letter obtain this?
- Is the whole letter professionally presented?

Reports

- Is the organisation clear?

- Are your headings effective?
- Have you been consistent?
- Are your lists in good order?
- Have you 'topped and tailed' it – contents, cross-references, etc?

Faxes/e-mails

- Is this the best form of communication for the job, or is it too informal?
- Has the medium affected your text – lost accents, poor reproduction, etc.?
- Are you sure the message has got through?
- Do you need to keep a copy?
- Have you expressed your ideas well, despite the informality of the medium?